Heart Sounds

Original cover art by Hayley Frazier.

ISBN-13: 978-0615964386
ISBN-10: 0615964389

To Mom, for keeping me grounded.

"*Music was my refuge. I could crawl into the space between the notes and curl my back to loneliness.*"

-Maya Angelou

INTRODUCTION

I'm not of the belief that one's teenage years are the best years of one's life, but they're not the worst either. My teenage years have transformed me, from a short kid with very few defined likes and dislikes, to a still pretty short young woman with far too many opinions.

But regardless of the quality of these years, I've documented them here. This book you hold in your very hands, I've stressed over, cried over, talked excitedly to my friends and family over. And now it's yours to do what you want with it.

I know one day, I will probably look back on this book with a bittersweet combination of shame and nostalgia. I will read over the lines once thought to be profound, with derision for my teenage self. In a way, this collection is a letter to my past self and my future self. And to you, dear reader. I hope you can relate to my experiences, and if not, that's okay too. And now, I present to you, *Heart Sounds*.

Best,
Hayley Elizabeth Thorpe

Table of Contents

Three

Four

These Little Words

My words are yours to hold.
They will haunt you until you
are no longer able to draw breath.
The ones who mourn your downfall
will be the ones left unaware
of your terminal infamy.

And they will write these cleverly
crafted, scathing, one-liners on your
tombstone, and those words will be
the truest ones that anyone has ever read.

The engraving will wear away
with time, but one thing
will remain. These will be
the only words
spoken to undo you.

One

November 19th, 1995

I am from the scuffed charm bracelet,
from the beaten up journal, carried
everywhere, that holds every thought.

I am from the small house near the busy
street, from the small cramped bedroom,
with walls plastered with posters
of rock stars, revered like gods.

I am from the daisies, the tulips,
the roses, the Impatiens, the Dahlias

I am from Lost River
and Smart Ass, from
Karen and Stephen,
and Tori and Hayley Bug.

I am from the tattered
and torn favorite novel.
From the Binky Fairy and
Mr. Tooth Decay. I am from
the Orioles and the Ravens,
cauliflower and cheese, and
Jello salad. I am from
Great Aunt Sally's dinner table.

December, 2009

I.

The eve of my best friend's
birthday party, and
There's a threat of a blizzard.
Snowpocalypse,
that's what they're calling it.
I wanted to stay the night anyway.
The next morning, both my parents
had to come get me, the snow so heavy
and thick around my little suburban world
was still coming down.

II.

My orthopedist's name
is Doctor Keane, but
mentally I refer to him
as Doctor Peachy Keane.
He's nice enough, except
he said I'd be rid of my brace
today. But still the sting of the
nearly-one-month-old sprain
twists in my ankle, like a small,
angry cobra. And now everyone
asks me, *you're still wearing that?*

As if my healing process isn't
going fast enough for them.
I grit my teeth around the
ever-present pain,
and now the nausea,
a stomach bug maybe.
I'd puked early this morning,
or late last night.
I can't skip the concert, I'll fail.
At least, that's what I told myself.
So I stood on those damned risers,
trying to lean on the back row,
While looking like I wasn't. We didn't go
to the Double T Diner that night
like we usually did, after every concert.

III.

That year, I was the token Scrooge
I only begrudgingly went downstairs
to open presents. I fell incidentally
into the Christmas Spirit.

IV.

People can only affect you
if you let them. I guess
that was true with you.

I marveled over you.
With all the unhappiness
floating around the world
like nearly invisible dust particles,
you were there, with your smile.
I was never the Scrooge again.

V.

January looms ahead, unforgiving.
And something else, *Carver Auditions*.
An event that was spoken in caps,
an invoice from reality, one I just
can't ignore. Subtly telling me to
get a move on with my life.
And also, my best friend is
auditioning with me, and I
know we both can't
possibly make the cut.
But it's not January yet.
Things haven't changed.
I can stay ensconced
in my safe little world, for now.

Fall, 2010

I remember the fall mornings
that were cold enough for winter,
head resting on the shoulder
of a new friend, found in
the peeling green seats
of a bold yellow bus
that took me away
for seven precious hours.

I remember the phone
buzzing against my bedside table,
jolting me awake. And the
pop punk that helped me
spring into action. Melodies
that now have a scent,
like fruity perfume
and hash browns, and a taste,
like mocha iced coffee.

I remember the hallway
with the downward slope
where the light slowly
became dimmer, as did
the one in my eyes.
The hallway where
kisses were stolen,

alliances were formed
and hearts were claimed.

I remember every moment
until it got too cold, and
reality became hazy, clouds formed
by huffing exhales, obscuring,
until the cast of characters
was nearly unrecognizable.

November 9th, 2011

We
have made
a world of our
own. a world where
nurses stick you several
times and you thank them for
doing so, even as your veins begin
to ache. a feat you never before would
have thought possible. a world where quiet
conversations are meaningless to the ones
outside your window. a world in which
food is ordered, but is never eaten.
a world where a reflection writes
a paragraph, an essay. a world
where everything is white
until you start
bleeding.

August 10th, 2012

I can't go to space,
can't walk freely on the moon.
I've just realized this.

Want to know something?
I can't scuba dive either.
Stupid damn pressure

Not sleeping is like
being in a different world.
Not sure I like it.

March 20th, 2013

I.

The bass pumping through
the Recher Theatre and into me,
like the blood in my veins.
I cup my hands, as if to
keep the feeling there,
A lightning bug, caught
between my palms.
Jumping up and down,
although my legs ache.
Screaming The Summer Set's
lyrics, although I can't hear
my own voice.

II.

I heard that the Recher is closing down
next month, but it doesn't matter.
Tonight belongs to me, and to
the other fans, who've counted down
from the day they bought their tickets
until tonight. Coming from all different
neighborhoods, in all different towns.
Some of the more dedicated fans,
from different states altogether.

III.

Everything so vibrant and sensory,
I can't breathe or see or think.
But maybe that's okay,
because right now, I exist.

IV.

Everything seems to sweat, even the walls.
I think I might go deaf, or lose my voice
one day. Time seems to stop, in this place.
It doesn't exist in the normal way.
It doesn't matter, because nothing is
scheduled. No one's expecting you to do
anything at a certain time, you're just here,
and that's enough for everyone there.

April 7th, 2013

Look to the sky, as if
your mistakes are fireworks,
you watch as they explode
with color and light,
and then disappear.

As if your shortcomings
were caused by someone else
and you're simply watching
the tragically beautiful results.

Things are about to change
but you don't want them to.
So you sit here and pretend
that time is yours to hold onto.

Autumn

Fall is the red of your bloodshot eyes,
the chocolate of your hair as it darkens
from lack of sun exposure, instead, days
are spent inside scrawling in a notebook
or typing manically. Fall is the green of
the trees, replaced by yellows and reds and
oranges, the denim of back-to-school jeans.

Fall is the white of school papers
flying, as they slip from the confines
of your already overstuffed binder.
It's the peach of the cool setting sun.
Fall is the tan of your skin, slowly paling,
the blue of the ink stains in your journal

It is the light blue pills that you must
take to try and get rid of the ache inside
of you. Fall is the aquamarine eyes that
fade to grey. Fall is the magenta sky of the
morning, having to rise before the sun.

The Perks of Being a Wallflower

When I was fourteen
and a freshman, my
senior mentor told me to read
The Perks of Being a Wallflower.
and I bought a copy
from Barnes and Noble
because she was older
and I believed she was
right about everything.

When I was fifteen
and still a freshman,
I tried to read
The Perks of Being a Wallflower.
And I didn't like it
because I didn't know who
the main character was writing to
and that bothered me.

When I was sixteen
and a sophomore,
I gave away my copy of
The Perks of Being a Wallflower
to my best friend.
She wanted to borrow it,
and then she wanted
to keep it, and I let her

because she was
right about everything.

When I was seventeen
and a junior, alone,
in my room, I watched
The Perks of Being a Wallflower.
Because my mom and sister
had rented it. And it changed me.
And I downloaded the book
onto my iPhone, and read
approximately half of it,
before I got bored.

And again, when I was seventeen,
almost a senior,
I again bought
The Perks of Being a Wallflower
from the same Barnes and Noble.
And I read it, and as I read,
I finally realized who
Charlie was writing to.
And I wished I had read it
when I was a freshman
because so many things
would've made sense

When I was almost eighteen,
finally a senior

I finally finished
The Perks of Being a Wallflower.
And I cried because
Charlie was leaving me
all alone again, and
I wondered where he was now.
And then I remembered,
he's another character
that someone else created
that came to life in my own mind.
And I was okay.

Witch Hunt

God will give you blood to drink
and one can only hope that
that will be the fate that awaits you.

I may not be headed to
sit among saints and apostles,
but I can say for certain
that neither are you.

No, your final resting place
lies farther down, where not
even your clever lines can save you.

Biology

I don't know how to explain
the lightness in my stomach,
when you tossed me a bag
of Skittles, my favorite,
as you knew.

How does one account for
the heat, like sunshine,
that rained down on
my bare shoulders?
It was the first day of
spring, and I was wearing
my new strapless dress,
and I looked up to find you
drawing me how you saw me.

I struggled to rationalize
the iced coffee and french fries,
that you paid for, since I forgot
to bring money.

I will listen to that song
that you said was your
favorite, hearing your voice
in the refrain.

I will search for what

you found in it, since
it doesn't sound
the same to me
anymore.

Two

M.H.

Paper and pen, wielded as weapons.
A torn notebook, a sparkle in her eye.
Glancing around the food court, she sighs.
Of her charm, I am endlessly fond.
We talk about life until the sun has gone.
I toss out the half-eaten food I bought.
Instead, lean in, to hear her thoughts.
Just a quiet piece of her to get me by
An exchange of goods, a CD, a book.
I lean back as we discuss movie plots.
I hold this moment in my own palm.
We speak in a code, in lyrics and jokes
At last we depart, I am happy for now.
She bids me farewell with a quirk of brow.

M.H. II

Time seems to change
in the sanctuary of her home.
The excitement of a new friend,
mugs filled with hot chocolate
topped with whipped cream.
Cheese pizza, *The Polar Express*,
Spin and *Alternative Press*,
arguments over the exact
meaning of that one song.

An afternoon spent in the basement,
With t-shirts, spray paint, sharpies.
iPod speakers blaring My Chemical
Romance's entire discography.

Or maybe with a movie, she let me choose,
so I made her watch *A Clockwork Orange*.
Projected onto the white sheet
hanging on the wall. Her mom
incidentally had veggie burgers
for me in the freezer.

Here, there is nowhere to go,
Nowhere to rush off to,
Nothing pressing to do.
Just her and I, and my own
admiration for her.

A.W.G.

In these moments,
He's the only one
That can understand.
He writes the lyrics,
And they are tattooed
On your heart, spray-painted
Onto your soul.

His songs pull you up
Off of the ground,
Holding your hand,
Giving you the courage
To keep marching on.

Forget the people
Who have wronged you,
Press backspace,
Until they are no longer
Characters in the story,
The story of your life.

L.E.

My life with you
was erratic,
unpredictable.
I kept my heart
dangling on my sleeve
and a goodbye
prepared just for you,
lingering on my lips.
Waiting for the day
you'd forget about me
and move on.

It was easier
that way.
I didn't have
to get hurt,
and you didn't
have to feel bad.
Not that you would
anyway, because
at any moment,
you'd no doubt
disappear.

Some days, I'd find
comfort
in your presence,
in the way your

brown eyes stayed
on me, connecting with
my own green ones.
And other times,
I felt like
an intruder
in my own life,
like this idyllic
everyday life
was meant
for someone
else.

My life without you
was safe, grounded
predictable. I enjoyed
the luxury of boredom,
counting up the days
on my fingers and toes,
losing track of the hours,
spent in real time
until you'd fall back to me.

L.E. II

When you leave,
be sure to lock the door.
Take your saccharine
sweet smirk, your
bright eyes, your
perpetually disheveled
post-summer hair.

You can keep all the nights
I spent in my bedroom,
shielding myself from the cold
with blankets and
college sweatshirts,
only to be treated to
your equally chilly moods.
Words that could cut
like an icicle.

You say it wasn't me,
you chalked it all
to circumstance.
But who can know
when you'd gladly
lie for nothing.

All I asked for
was a part of you,

an atom, a thought.
Something,
concrete or not.
When you couldn't
even give me that,
I should have
said goodbye.

Elaine

She's not the same person
that she was a month ago
or last week, or even
just yesterday.

What would she have said
to herself right now?
What would she have done?

Would she have combed
through her own graying
blonde hair, straightened
the collar of her worn polo,
and made things right?
Or would she just have
walked away?

She was once a mother,
a grandmother, a hostess.
But now she perches timidly
on her own couch, unsure
of the role she plays
in her own world.

The piano in the corner,
a metaphor of her own life.
What once stood tall with grandeur,
now sits, abandoned in the corner,

waiting for something to be different.

You

You had no life left,
so you took away mine.

Your soul was as dark
as winter nights
spent alone, so you
blackened my own.

You were bored,
so with one fell swoop,
you reached out, with
hands like gnarled claws
and took away from me,
everything that I had worked for.

You made me hurt,
so you could feel better
about whatever it was
that made you do this
to me in the first place.

At the end of it,
you weren't thinking
about me at all, you
were simply thinking
of your next paycheck

even though I'm the one
that truly ended up paying

for what you did.

I was just a consequence,
of my own youth, and
the actions of someone
who should've known better.

It must be nice, not to have
to think about anyone else.

Harvey

He thought you were
a miracle.
A man who
had seen war,
and ugliness,
thought you,
a stoic bundle
of blankets and
tangled limbs,
were incredible.
Imagine that.

There was a time,
a time before you
can even remember,
when he could speak.
It was a time before
the tracheostomy,
and Chronic Obstructive
Pulmonary Disease that
turned him into a
helpless man, but a
hardened one
just the same.
You used to sit
on his lap, but
now you keep
your distance.

You spent your
last days with him
playing cards, but not
with each other, eating
identical bowls of
Rice Krispies, a
favorite cereal
which you shared,
occasionally, he'd
look up at you, wearily.

You shared his dislike
of orange marmalade,
but you wouldn't know
why he hated it until
it was too late.

7-Up was his
favorite soda.
You ordered it
on the plane ride
home, a tribute
to his memory.

By the time you
left him behind
for the last time,
he was already gone,
it was just that
no one knew it yet.

When Someone Likes You

You view the world
through rose colored glasses,
and you try to view yourself
the way they might see you.

You are described as a goddess,
but you can never stare
into the mirror long enough
to see it that way.

Instead you see a girl, staring
back at you with blood red eyes,
claws where bitten fingernails
should be, and hair that
only Medusa could appreciate.

Then came the day when
you painted the roses, red
onto porcelain doll arms
and legs, because the roses
inside of you had finally
frosted over.

The Elf

Uncle Carl had told us that
there was an elf that lived
in the tree that separated
the backyard from the alley.

So, we waited, with hope
on our breaths, hope that
smelled like melons, and could
set fire to the entire yard
all in one little puff.

I had a half-eaten pack
of strawberry gum in my
sticky pink fist. I was chewing
one piece as it slowly stained
my tongue with pinky red dye.

I tap on the small wooden block
that acts as the elf's front door,
and then we wait. We wait for his
croaky voice to ring in the air
from somewhere up above,
hoping we'd been good enough
to deserve a showering of candy.

The door is split in half, from the time
we'd tried to break it down when we didn't
receive our candy. Or maybe when

we were curious and we wanted to come
inside to visit our dear friend, Mr. Elf.

I try to push away the nagging doubt
that lingers in my mind. The voice
sounds like it's coming from the garage
not ten feet away from us.

I don't say anything.
No one would believe
the word of a four year old
who'd been gullible enough
to believe in candy-bearing elves
that live in rotting trees.

These Ghosts

I.

You made your marks on me, but
purposefully left no trace.
Save for the duct tape bracelet
you made me, that I tried to throw away,
but could only make it to my closet,
where on the teal carpeted floor,
lies a tattered shoe box, full of things
from my previous lives; hospital bracelets,
photos from my first summer at camp,
tickets to the minor league baseball games.
You joined the legion of ghosts.
You are now just one of them.

II.

You never held me, as if
I was made of porcelain,
even though you knew
I was just as breakable.
Instead your claws cut
and your teeth snapped
and tore at skin and cartilage.
And when it was over,
you became just like everyone else
that I had let inside of me.

III.

If I walk away, I'm a fool,
but if I stay, my self-respect
drops by the hour, so that
I can never win, and you
never have to lose.

The Dog That Followed Her

Glance behind you
and there he is, his
little legs struggling
to keep up with
your much longer ones.

He's like a duck, trailing
after anything that resembles
a maternal figure, those big brown
eyes crying "are you my mother?"

He stands by the door
expectantly, already knowing
he's coming along.

Wait a moment,
there's someone
across the street.
You know he'd
chase after them
if you released him now.

Outside, off the stoop
in front of the house,
he's there, as always.

He beats you to the car and
he runs mini-marathons

around the driveway while
you're waiting for your mother
to come out with the keys.

Passenger side door opens
he leaps onto the front seat,
executing leaps and bounds
from the driver's seat to yours
and then back again the other way.

Mother arrives, you get settled in.
Caringly you wrap a towel
around his long, lean body,
to shield him from the cruel
early morning weather that
just isn't meant for dachshunds.

Engine starts and you're off.
He perks up, propping himself
against the door, to better see
out of the car window.

The wonderment is clear
in his glistening brown eyes.
Another adventure, the drive
to the bus stop. He expects to be
invited along, but still, it entertains him.

Three

Remember

I

It was cold today, too cold.
I thought of you, the day we met
did you think of me? Why would you?

II

that summer evening,
I chased after the fireflies
until they all disappeared,
as you fumbled to take a picture
with the old camera that I coveted.

III

that one year,
I told you to
forget my birthday.
You did, and I cried.

IV

that day, I walked right past
you and didn't say a word.
you wouldn't remember that.
You looked right through me.

V

you went to the end
of the earth, just to
see me smile. I don't
recall that either.

VI

you played me that
one song, whose name
I could never remember.
I said it was deep and
gushed at how good the
bass line was. I lied.

VII

that one night, we stayed up till five,
just to see what would happen.
We cheated, it wasn't morning.
The sun hadn't even risen yet.
But it was good enough for us.

VIII

I threw sticks at you
from my perch in the
"Girls' Tree"? In my language,

that meant I love you.

IX

that one day I didn't feel
like speaking, so we passed
notes until I did. Thanks for that.

X

on our last day, I clung
to your short stature,
crying. I'm sorry it ended.

Teenage Dirtbag

White is not a color,
according to the stoic boy,
with hunched shoulders
and shaggy hair that hangs
in his deadened blue eyes.

Those eyes follow you
even when he's not
in the room with you.
They criticize you,
making you think twice.

He's not reading poetry,
so much as performing,
as if the words were written
in the back of his mind,
instead of on paper.

Notes passed back
and forth, between the two
like a ping pong ball.

Back and forth, every day.
Why couldn't you have believed him?
His breath, so close to yours,
carried the truth into you.

He begged you, plainly,
don't let me disappear.
But you let him become
another story, another rumor.

Eyes

If you had only
looked into my
eyes,
you would've seen
so much more.

You would've seen
the aftershock
of your words.

You would've seen
the battle flashbacks
of a hospital bed veteran.

The whites would have
showed you the volumes
of medicals bills that
I tried not to worry about.

In the pupils, you'd see
the inky black of your name,
written a thousand times
in my psychiatric records,
that cited you as
my reasoning for being crazy.

And then you might've

noticed the disparity in size
of one pupil and the other,
a physical feature, that
someone else had
to point out to me.

If you had even bothered
to take another look,
you would've seen the story,
the one that cast you,
deservingly, as the villain,
the one I told many times,
to many experts, and then
was promptly told to forget.

When I am Dead

When I am dead, my dearest,
Grieve for me, day and night.
Toss and turn with regret
Of what you could have told me.
Bury me next to a rose bush.
If there aren't any cemeteries
That have rose bushes in them,
Plant one. If that's against the law,
Too bad. I'm dead, so respect me.

Curl my hair in evening ringlets,
Fold my hands and let me hold
The bouquet of daisies.
Daisies are happy flowers, right?
Maybe you're happy that I'm dead

Worship me even after the grass grows
Overtop of the dirt where lies my remains
You'll still know where I am, even after
The tombstone breaks down, becoming
one with the dirt, drifting into the sea.

You'll still know where I used to lie,
because the grass might grow just a little
brighter. I hope it does.

And when the ocean tide blows in
A perfectly formed sea shell,
When the apple blossoms are
The perfect shades of pink and white
That's where I'll be.

The Stars

The stars, frozen, mid-tango
Will begin to dance
After you look away.
Stories end, with sunsets
Fallen leaves adore
The ground they lay on.
Life begins to pulse,
Wavering like
A dying heart.
Common sense
is the ottoman
you rest your feet on.
Some have forgotten
how to sink below
the raging, rushing tides.
And how to make sandcastles
from hopes and secrets.
Silence worms itself into the holes
Where inside jokes once nestled.
Good thing you don't have any feelings.

Dry Spell

If anyone asks,
I gave too much
And took too little.
I loved too hard, and fought,
but only when needed.

If anyone asks,
you're not as bad
as everyone says you are,
but the truth is, you
are your worst critic.

I walk with my head high,
with a constant need to be held,
curled up in my heart,
like a sleeping dog.

I search for something
profound, reading
between the lines,
analyzing the smoke
that weaves in and out
of the dark blue night sky.

The Sunday Paper

Forget about the bright
Sunday mornings,
The walls painted yellow,
the blank canvas
hidden behind your eyes.
Coffee cup held in shaking hands,
I long to hear something profound
from you. The scars have faded, but
you can still see them, Weaving lines
like a road map of where we've been.
If love did exist, I'd forgive you,
And we would laugh together
About the comics in the newspaper.
I'd pretend to hate your favorite,
But honestly, it makes you who you are.
And I'm just me, and I might forgive you.
Pretend for a second that we would last.

Recovery

Fighting the monsters
You thought you'd shrugged off,
The ones that linger
In your closet, under your bed,
Living off fear and negativity,
Clinging to the last of their lives,
Clawing you open, until you're raw.

Having to stand tall and be brave,
When others cower around you,
Paper cut-out soldiers
With their army bases
Made of fifty-two cards.

Under a thin facade lies
Their veiled cowardice.
And once you're strong,
You can never again be weak.

Things have come full circle now
The ghosts are pulling on your arms,
Into the past, into the future.
You just want to stay in the present
Stay grounded, stay real.

I Am

I want to be made of glass,
shiny, and smooth, and spotless,
but I'd only shatter when I fall
out of the china cabinet.

I want to be paper and pen.
I want to be permanent,
I want to last forever.
If only I could.

I want to be magazines,
glossy, fleeting. I want
to be the hourglass figure
gracing the cover.

I wish the world
would open its eyes
to me, open its arms
to my pain, and embrace
me, like a warm summer
spotlight at noon.

I wish my mistakes
would fall off of me,
down like droplets
of water after a shower.

I want to have wisdom
that I bury in the sand
with the toe of my shoe
that grows into something
worth living for.

I pray for ingenuity to
rest its wings on the
headboard of my bed
and whisper clever lines
to my sleeping form, so
when I awaken, I can
be better than I am.

I beg for fear and
anxiety to quit
their day jobs
and give me
one night off.

I wish that old demons
would take an early retirement,
because even as I take steps
farther and farther away,
even as I outrun them by
miles upon miles, I still
need to look over my shoulder,
to ensure that they stopped
hiding in my shadow.

Therapy

You've never known
an unfamiliar room, a bed
that's been slept in by many,
and a pillow that crinkles
like newspaper.

You wouldn't recognize
the cold stares of the
experts, those who
are older, and
supposedly wiser.

You would not accept,
the proverbial dirt, filling
your lungs as you tried
to make sense of a world
that kicked you further
into the underworld
before you'd had the chance
to stand again.

You'd never get to see
the wars waging
behind the stoic mask
of someone who knows
to never start fires
she can't put out.

You've never painted
the scenery, mapped
the choreography,
down to all the footfalls
and the final exhales,
until the lust for execution
kills you inside.

You'd never be
able to rationalize
a room meant for two
but inhabited by many.
Demons taking their
rightful places
around your bed.

Drowned

the device is just
plastic and rubber
with an over-inflated
self esteem. funny how
that's what keeps you alive.

you're used to lifting up
one section of your hair
for complete strangers,
so they can feel the bump
nestled beneath your skin.

you know an alphabet soup
of acronyms, a knowledge
unlike any party trick.

you've learned to distinguish,
with a small percentage of error,
between a headache that will lead
to MRI's, hospital stays, surgeries,
and one that just needs to be slept off
in a dark room with some Advil.

your childhood nightmares
consisted of basketballs
flying at your head

I Only Want to Cut You Open

I only want to cut you open,
Invert your insides, so that
Your heart is on the outside
To rot and decay, for someone
To take a swing at if they
Felt wronged by you.
Or maybe if you just
Happened to be in their way.

You'd scream and moan
And wretch and cry in pain
You'd yell in anguish, and
They'd all scoff at you.

Who are you, they'd say.
Who are you to think
You can stake a claim
To experiencing your own pain.

After centuries of hate and
Hurt and war and death,
Your pain is unimportant.

So they will silence you,
Because in your piercing youth
You couldn't possibly begin
To even fathom what

Real pain is.

And maybe after
Falling to the floor,
Your knees breaking
In time with your exposed heart,
You could begin to see it too.

Paroxetine

The dreaded white pills
course through the bloodstream,
mechanizing emotion,
synthesizing expression.
I want to laugh uncontrollably,
just to cry inconsolably,
to feel something;
see something; do something.
I want my emotions to be mine.
I want them to be created
here, in my mind, and not
in a factory, by a strange worker
or an even stranger machine.
Because they weren't there
on the day when things fell apart.
They weren't there on the night
that I put it all back together.
They can keep their pills,
their artificial solutions.

China Doll

I paint my face
to look like the China doll
whose face I cracked
and legs I shattered
when I dropped her
in the driveway.

Because no one wants
to see the battle, only
the victory matters.
No one wants to see
the pain, only how
it made you be stronger,
fight harder.

I am little more than a name,
ink on paper, numbers.
And when it comes down to it,
I'm no different than any of them.

The things that my application
would not be complete without,
cannot be transcribed to paper.

Failure is a daily occurrence
that does not lend itself
to essay form.

Aren't We Just Clever?

Breathing fire to the starry night
Cigarettes hanging languidly from
Dirty fingers, blistered from the days
Ecstasies and sorrows alike,
For we are the ones who stand and
Gawk when kingdoms fall to ruin.

Heavens open up, and gods gaze down,
I don't think I can be myself today.
Just the words you said to me,
Knowing everything comes to an end.
Lust made us glassy-eyed, and
Made us think it was something bigger.

Anxiety

There's a monster in my chest.
It sits there, next to my heart,
unwilling to move, digging
its grimy talons, into my
no longer thick skin.
It hangs on tight
with no hope of extraction.

Unable to be popped,
like a zit.
Won't show up in a biopsy.
and
don't even think
about trying to freeze it.
It runs at temperatures
that rival the Arctic
and compete
with my own heart.

Every day, it perches there
probably chopping off
days from my life.

They See Your Eyes

Snow brings
ice cold reverie.
Darkness encourages
demons that float
from the smoke
of your breath,
and then they're
gone, ethereal,
like comets.
They wait
to possess
a human form.

Four

Le Mars, Iowa

grass under my feet,
damp and fresh
the smell of minty herbs
from somewhere.

the laughter of my
cousins and me
the banter of my
big happy family
grandma is making
jello salad and baked beans
several coolers
full of soda pop
and ring-shaped ice cubes
worn as frozen jewelry

we beg and plead
to go to the big playground
the ice cream parlor
or the snow cone stand
just one more time before,
tearfully, I must hop on a plane
and go back to where I belong.

lawn chairs
spread in a circle
everyone's together

for now

how much longer
until they go their separate ways
back to Florida, South Dakota,
Nebraska, and more states to which
I've never been, leaving sorrow hanging
like the imaginary laundry
on the long, unused clothesline

Art Class

You shouldn't run with scissors,
Everyone knows that. But also,
you shouldn't give your heart
to the boy with inky black eyes,
whose opacity only reflected
your own flaws back to you.

You shouldn't befriend the girl,
who, at eleven, looks like she
could be a Victoria's Secret angel,
where you look like the girl
in the makeover movie, except
instead of smoke and mirrors,
hipster glasses, and ill-fitting clothes,
it's only you, and it always will be.

You share the same first name,
and that's where the similarity ends,
when she put pink streaks
in her hair, you called her brave.
When someone called
across the art room, that
the boy liked her, and they
subsequently went out,
you pretended to be happy
for her, and shrugged
when they broke up.

When he stands behind you
in line at the sink, paint
covering his hands, while
you rinse your palette,
you should ignore the
fire and ice in his gaze.
Frost was sort of right,
your world ends in both
of those things.

Epiphany

He's burning you
and freezing you simultaneously,
all with his eyes,
and yet you feel nothing.

Nothing but your feet becoming
ensconced in cotton clouds.
Your heart and your stomach
clenching in unison, like a pair of fists,
every time his spider web lashes
drift across her infant smooth cheeks.

His eyes are so clear, seeing
into the very core of you.
They're the kind of color
you try to put a name to,
but, try as you might,
when you're alone in bed
that night, you cannot recall
the exact blend of colors.

You may as well be a little kid,
trying to capture air in a jar
to give to your mother,
just to show how
grown up you are.

Hide and Seek

I wish I could tell you
in my own words,
in twelve point
Times New Roman,
double spaced format,
 what everything means.

There are words ones
that crawl inside of me,
etching deep thoughts
into my bones, tracing each
column of my spinal cord.

The ones you can see
traces of at the bottom of
my morning mug of coffee.

The ones you can smell
among the midday petrichor.
The ones that won't leave,
even at night, when I am
vulnerable in my bed, like
a rose before a frost.

Until I am left trying to
get things exactly right
on paper, but I can't.

And I never will.

Inner Harbor

Our shelter for the afternoon
from the Baltimore chill
was a cool alcove
in Barnes and Noble.

We sat cross-legged,
reading books we
didn't intend to purchase,
and listening to your
new CD by The Strokes,
Someday blaring through
your over-sized headphones.

We ventured out again,
this time to the thrift store
you wanted to check out.

This Car

The passenger seat has known
many mornings, afternoons,
and nights.

I remember the late afternoon
one of the big kids pushed me down,
disguising her actions as a friendly hug,
even though she'd always hated me.

There was the pink and blue
knit hat, with ear flaps and
braided string that hung down
to rest on my shoulders.

My mom kept taking it off,
pulling over to examine
the bump on the back of my
head. I never wore it
again, threw it in my closet,
wanting to forget
that whole afternoon.

I remember the late
morning, my first day
of eighth grade, when
I begged my mom
to just take me home,

so I could eat fast food.
I'd try to forget the sound
of the popular girls' laughter,
not knowing that in four years,
I'd forget all their names.

I remember the late night,
coming home from Ocean City
the summer before freshman year.
I'd made my mom pick me up
early from my friend's family's
shared vacation house.
I'd been trying to be an adult,
brush off the homesickness.

The van has known many
road trips, many grocery store
parking lots. The passenger seat,
bearing the weight of a dozen
breakups, and falling-outs.

It has grown tired of the
drama of everyday life.
It's ready to retire,
as soon as we let it.

Dalliance

The crooked,
imperfect teeth
are framed
by swollen lips.

The eyes are like
the Christmas lights
that stay on the trees
all year long,

He's staring at you,
expecting. But nothing
comes to mind.

And suddenly you don't
want the traitorous words
to ram past the barricades
of your worried lips.

It would ruin the
moment anyway.
So, you decide to remain
silent until the roaring

of lions, tigers,
and bears, swelling
around the two of you

fills the negative space
between his words and
where yours would've been.

Brain Surgery

Some days, my illness
sits upon my head
and buzzes in my ear,
like a mosquito,
vying for my attention.

Some days, it tugs me down,
until I'm in my bed, in the dark
with the curtains drawn shut,
exactly where it wanted me.

Some days, it brings headaches
that blind me for a moment,
pains that might've struck down
Atlas himself, except for the fact
that the shoulders that must bear
this Herculean effort are too weak
and due to break at any moment.

Some days, it tugs on my arms
like a small child, wanting to
show me something. But
all it shows me is a hospital bed,
that drags me down lower
and lower, until I can feel
dirt piling on top of me.

Some days, it burns
my throat, like a dragon
slumbering in my stomach.
Dysphonia plagues my nightmares.

And some days, it does
absolutely nothing to me.
It lulls me into the false sense
of security that is synonymous
with my definition of normalcy.

Radio City Music Hall

Nestled in the comfortable seats
of the Showplace of the Nation,
we are four of 6,015, my aunt,
her friend, and her friend's daughter,
who was about two months older than me.

In the golden glow of the
cavernous theatre, I remove
the two coats, scarf, and hat
I wore to shield myself
from the unforgiving
New York City air.

I marvel at the Rockettes,
their long, slender, shimmering
legs, sheathed in gauzy,
ethereal stockings.
They seem to kick
higher than the skyscrapers
just outside this
warm, festive
sanctuary.

Their high heeled
tap shoes make
a satisfying "clack"

with each footfall.

You Do, You Don't

I remember the night
we stood in your bedroom,
I read over your shoulder
as you showed me
your favorite childhood poems.

I wanted nothing more
to take you in my arms,
and just hold you, keep you
away from yourself,
and from the world,
as it crumbled around us.

After the night of scaring
each other and ourselves
with videos and stories,
we brought in the New Year.

At the time, we had everything,
and we had nothing to lose.
I rode home to the sound
of soft piano, and a comforting
voice like Dove chocolate,
crooning in my ear through
my iPod, thinking back
to last night, how you
almost made me forget

the boy with the pretty eyes
and the long silky hair.
almost.

Here's to You

This goes to the afternoons
with pop punk blasting
from the speakers
in my best friend's bedroom.

To the nights spent
staying out too late,
few and far between,
but they mattered
in their own way.

To the afternoon we
laid on the cold tile
of the hallway floor
and it felt like something
from a hit teen movie.

To the rides in friend's cars
and friend's parents' cars.
I will remember most
the red convertible
that shouldn't have
been able to fit all of us.

To hugs that
lasted too long.
And kisses,

imagined but
never acted on.

To the songs,
and books, and movies,
and poems
that mattered.
They seemed important,
and they changed
the way we saw things.

ACKNOWLEDGEMENTS

I'd like to thank Karen Thorpe, the one I call Mommy.

I'd like to thank my family and friends of my family.

Thank you to the Literary Arts class of 2014, my second family, and to Mr. Jay Imbrenda, Ms. Suhaila Tenly, and Ms. Suzanne Supplee, and also Ms. Madeleine Mysko, and Ms. Linda Chambers. You all have given me confidence, strength, and love, and I now feel safe to move on, but I will never forget.

Many thanks to my cover artist, Hayley Frazier, for going above and beyond my expectations.

Thanks to my lovely, fantastic friends:

Joey Fay, thank you for being there for me, with smiles and hugs and advice.

Maddie Hardy, we've been through so much together and I don't know what the future holds for us, but I know if you're there, it'll be an adventure.

Anna Zacharias, thank you for listening, and for giving me advice whenever I needed it.

Thanks to my hydrocephalus family, for sharing my pain.

Thanks to my church, to Pastor Clara, and Pastor Courtney, to Natalie Brosh.

To my favorite writers: Jodi Picoult, Jonathan Larson, Noah Haidle, Billy Collins, Ellen Hopkins, and Lisa McMann.

Thanks to anyone who's read my writing for me, or inspired poetry.

Most importantly, to all the bands and musicians who have serenaded me through life's best and worst moments, but especially: All Time Low, My Chemical Romance, The Bigger Lights, The Summer Set, Cassadee Pope, and more.

Without all of you, I have no idea where I'd be.

ABOUT THE AUTHOR

Hayley is a native to Baltimore, Maryland. She has a penchant for yoga pants and Starbucks lattes, and hates when people crack their knuckles.

When Hayley's not being a master of the pen, she enjoys reading, watching movies, spending time with her family and friends, as well as playing with her three dogs.

www.ingramcontent.com/pod-product-compliance
Lightning Source LLC
Chambersburg PA
CBHW071903020426
42331CB00010B/2644